Spo... ...zil

Collins

Brazil on the map

Brazil is the biggest country in South America and the fifth largest in the world. It covers three different time zones, so when it's 9 o'clock in Rio de Janeiro, it's 8 o'clock in Manaus.

Most of Brazil is just south of the **equator**, so it has a tropical **climate**. The Amazon rainforest covers around half of the country, and the mighty Amazon River runs across the entire northern part of Brazil. Many tourists visit Brazil to see the rainforest and river, to see the beautiful beaches of Rio de Janeiro, to watch football and to join in carnival celebrations.

Venezuela

Colombia

The Equator

Manaus

Amazon River

South America

Peru

Brazil

Brasília

Bolivia

Rio de Janeiro

São Paulo

Paraguay

PACIFIC OCEAN

Argentina

Uruguay

ATLANTIC OCEAN

rainforest

time zones

This is the Brazilian flag. The green background represents the rainforests of Brazil. The yellow diamond is the colour of the gold that was discovered in Brazil in the 18th century.

On the flag is the **motto**, "*Ordem e Progresso*". This means "Order and Progress".

The money used in Brazil is the *real*. There are 100 *centavos* in one *real*.

▪▪▪▶ **Fast fact**

There are more than 4,000 airports in Brazil!

A people's history

Groups of **native** Indians have lived in Brazil for thousands of years, but Pedro Álvares Cabral, a Portuguese explorer and nobleman, was the first person from Europe to reach Brazil.

He arrived on 22 April 1500, on his way to India. After 1530, more people from Portugal and the rest of Europe followed him and settled in Brazil.

As more and more Portuguese came to live in Brazil, Portuguese eventually became the **official** language.

⤳ Fast fact

The name Brazil comes from a redwood tree called *pau brasil*, which grows in forests on the Atlantic coast.

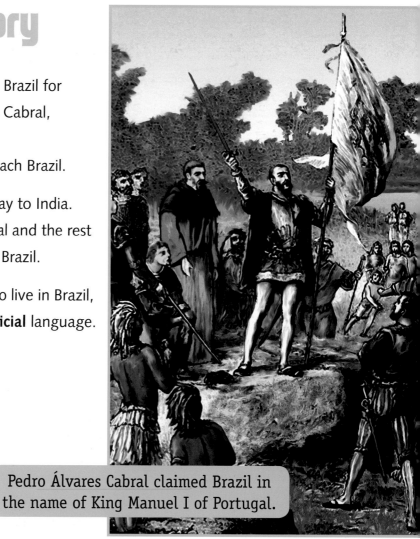

Pedro Álvares Cabral claimed Brazil in the name of King Manuel I of Portugal.

Settlers and slaves

The early **settlers** realised that the **fertile** land was just right for growing sugar cane. Sugar soon became the most important crop in Brazil and made many landowners very rich. The landowners didn't have enough local workers, so they brought over people from West Africa as slaves and forced them to work on the sugar plantations.

Between 1550 and 1850, about five and a half million slaves were brought to Brazil in ships. They were squashed together in appalling conditions. Around 660,000 died before they even got to Brazil. The slave ships were known as *"tumbeiros"* (coffin carriers).

Once in Brazil, slaves were poorly treated, and many didn't live beyond 30. Slavery was eventually **abolished** in 1888.

5

From Portuguese rule to republic

In 1549, a nobleman and soldier called Tomé de Sousa sailed to Brazil from Portugal to set up the first government. This meant that Brazil was now officially ruled by Portugal. The first capital city was Salvador, in the north-east.

On 7 September 1822, Portuguese prince, Dom Pedro, declared that Brazil should be **independent** from Portugal. Every year, 7 September is now known as Independence Day, and is a national holiday in Brazil.

Dom Pedro, the first Emperor of Brazil

Salvador

celebrating Independence Day in Salvador

In 1889, a new Brazilian **republic** was declared and the people could choose their own president. However, very few Brazilians were actually able to vote (many couldn't even read) so the country ended up being run by a small group of powerful people – landowners who'd become rich from growing coffee or farming cattle.

It wasn't until 1985 that *all* Brazilian people had the freedom to choose their own president.

⇒ **Fast fact**

Dilma Rousseff was the first female president of Brazil. She was elected in 2010, and again in 2014.

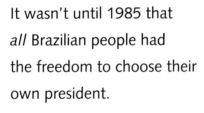

7

Brazil today

Today there are over 200 million people in Brazil. Many more of them live in cities than in the countryside. Almost half of the entire population live in the south-east, in São Paulo (the largest city in South America) and Rio de Janeiro.

1,200 kilometres inland from Rio is the capital, Brasília. It was **founded** in 1960 and is a modern city with many unusual and **eye-catching** buildings.

Over 40 million people live in the **sprawling** city of São Paulo.

Brasília Cathedral

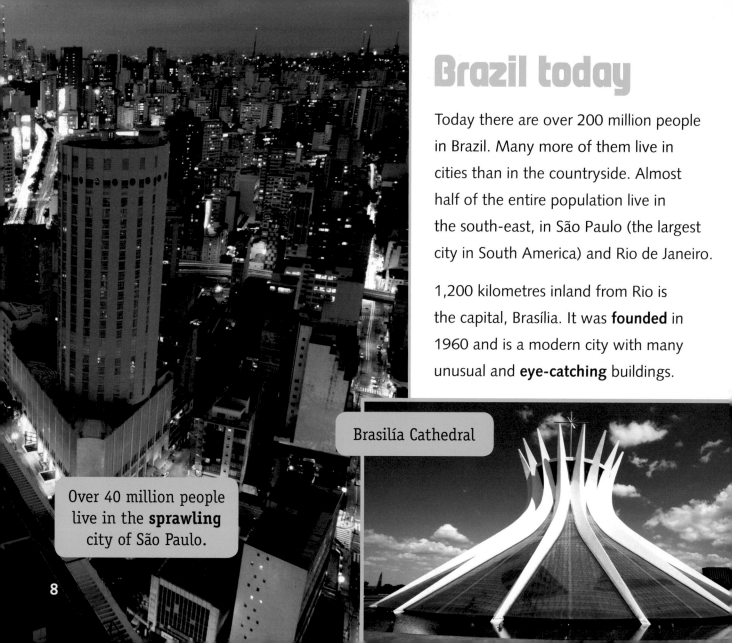

Favelas are towns on the edge of Brazil's big cities. When large groups of people moved away from the countryside looking for work, they couldn't afford to live in the city. Instead they built houses, **illegally**, often on steep hillsides, because the land there was free.

The houses are tightly packed together, with narrow streets between them. Some favelas still have no running water or electricity. However, in large *favelas* like Rocinha, in Rio de Janeiro, most houses have been rebuilt in concrete and brick, and there are schools, businesses and areas to play sport.

Over 100,000 people live in Rocinha. This is one-fifth of Rio's entire population.

9

Rio de Janeiro

Rio de Janeiro was the capital of Brazil for almost two centuries, from 1763 until 1960. It's a beautiful city with long, white, sandy beaches stretching along Guanabára Bay. Tijuca National Park comes right down into the city.

Tourists come to enjoy the beach life and to soak up the atmosphere of this bustling **metropolis** – the second largest in Brazil, with a population of over six million. A popular trip is to ride a cable car to the top of *Pão de Açúcar* (Sugarloaf Mountain).

⇒ Fast fact

Rio de Janeiro means "River of January". This is the name given to it by the Portuguese explorers who came here on 1 January 1502.

Hosting the world – twice!

In 2014, Rio was one of 12 cities in Brazil to host the FIFA World Cup tournament. Huge numbers of fans travelled from all over the world to Brazil for the football – and the party!

In 2016, Rio will be the home of the twenty-eighth Olympic Games – the first time the Games will have been held in South America. Rowing, sailing, athletics, canoeing and beach volleyball will take place at Rio's famous Copacabana beach.

The Maracanã Stadium in Rio de Janeiro is the largest in Brazil.

Sport

Football crazy!

Brazilians are passionate about football. They call their country "*O País do Futebol*" (the country of football). Brazilian football is known for its **flamboyant** style and rhythm. It's been called "Samba Soccer" – it's almost as if the players are dancing! Many of the world's greatest players have been, and are, Brazilian.

Pelé

Ronaldinho

Neymar

▪▪▪▶ **Fast fact**

Brazil has won the World Cup a record five times!

The Brazil Grand Prix

Motor racing is almost as popular in Brazil as football. The Formula One Grand Prix takes place in São Paulo every year, and drivers from all over the world race round the track at speeds of up to 360 kilometres per hour.

Brazil has produced many skilled racing drivers. The most famous are Nelson Piquet and Ayrton Senna. Piquet and Senna were both Formula One Champions three times. When Senna died in a race crash, over a million **grieving** fans took to the streets of São Paulo for his funeral.

Going to school

a public school in Rio de Janeiro

Life isn't all sport. Children start school at the age of six and stay until they are 14. Some children in poorer areas end up leaving before this so that they can get jobs to help their families.

There's a large number of children in Brazil, so in order to give everyone a chance to go to school, the day is divided into two or three sessions (these could be 7 o'clock in the morning to midday; midday to 5 o'clock in the afternoon and 5 o'clock in the afternoon to 10 o'clock at night). Pupils go to one of these sessions only, with younger ones going earlier in the day.

The main subjects at primary school are Maths, Geography, History, Science, Portuguese, Spanish, English and PE. After school, sports like football, handball, volleyball, tennis and athletics are played, and there are also chances to do music and drama.

Usually, there's no school at all during the months of January and July. The seasons in Brazil are different from those in Europe, so in January, it's very hot. In July, it's cooler – but still very warm!

⟶ **Fast fact**

12 October is Children's Day when children are given sweets and presents. Of course, they get a day off school!

a class in a *favela* in Rio de Janeiro, under a city overpass

Carnival: the biggest show on Earth!

Carnival is a huge part of Brazilian culture. It's a giant street party made up of noisy parades, dancers and musicians. People of all ages take part in this week-long celebration, and dress up in fantastic costumes. Visitors come from all over the world to see the famous carnivals in cities such as Rio and Salvador.

Costume makers work all year to create incredible outfits. Every year there's a different theme.

colourful costumes at the Salvador carnival

Samba

Samba is the most famous form of music and dance in Brazil. It's heard everywhere during carnival time as dancers and drummers from special clubs parade down the street.

Samba schools practise all year to compete for the huge honour of performing at the *Sambódromo* (a specially designed stadium) in Rio. Only 14 schools are chosen, so competition is fierce!

samba drummers and samba dancers

Fast fact

Samba originally comes from Africa, where drums are often used in music. It was made popular by African slaves.

Eating and drinking

Because Brazil is such a large country, with people living there from so many different cultures, its food is very **varied**. The long coastline and the huge number of fish in the Amazon River mean that fish and seafood are often used in cooking. Meals are very **sociable** and families make time to sit down together every day.

Breakfast

Coffee (children drink very milky coffee), bread or *pão de queijo* (puffy cheese rolls), cheese, ham and fruit like mango, pineapple or papaya.

Lunch or dinner

Rice, beans, salad, vegetables and chicken, pork or beef.

Sweet treats

Brigadeiros (little balls of cocoa powder, butter and condensed milk, rolled in chocolate sprinkles) are very popular for children's birthday parties.

Drinks

Brazil's climate means that tropical fruits are plentiful. Street stands sell fruit juices, coconut juice and smoothies.

⟹ Fast fact

In the 18th century a coffee bush was **smuggled** into Brazil from a neighbouring country. The climate in south-east Brazil is perfect for growing coffee beans and the coffee bush soon grew strong. Today, Brazil is the biggest producer of coffee in the world!

Amazing Amazon
The Amazon rainforest

This is the world's largest tropical rainforest. It covers nearly seven million square kilometres – more than half of this is in Brazil. It's home to an incredible number of plants and animals, including 2,000 types of tree and one-tenth of all animal species on the planet.

⇒ **Fast fact**

The canopy of the rainforest, formed by the top branches and leaves, is so thick that the ground below is in total darkness. When it rains it takes around ten minutes for the water to reach the ground!

Animals in the rainforest

The rainforest is a noisy, **humid** place, which buzzes with 2.5 million different insects. Bright green parrots, yellow-fronted toucans and scarlet macaws flap and screech in the tall trees. Giant, hairy, bird-eating Goliath tarantulas hide in deep burrows. Highly poisonous coral snakes slither along the forest floor. Jaguars stalk their prey from the tree tops.

Brazil has more kinds of monkey than any other country. Many people think that there are species of monkey in the rainforest that haven't been discovered yet.

Brazilian red tarantula

21

People in the rainforest

Imagine living in the hot, steamy climate of the rainforest. It's estimated that around 500 tribes of native Indians do. They survive by hunting with spears, fishing and **foraging**.

In the past, native Indians have been threatened by outsiders who wanted to take over their land for growing crops. Now, the government in Brazil keeps careful watch over the land where these tribes live, so that they can carry on with their lives without being disturbed.

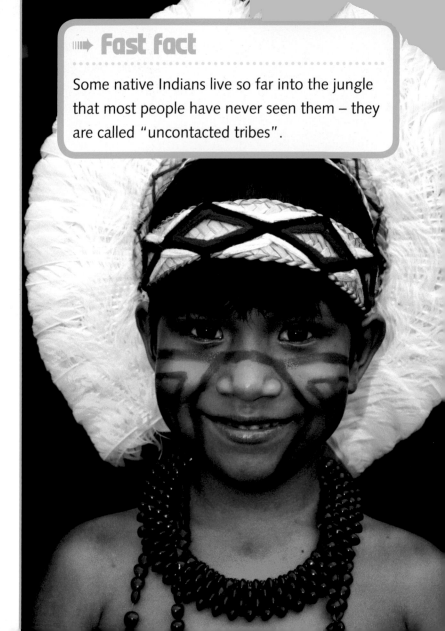

⟹ Fast fact

Some native Indians live so far into the jungle that most people have never seen them – they are called "uncontacted tribes".

The Amazon River

The Amazon River runs through the northern part of the rainforest. At 6,400 kilometres long, it's the world's second largest river, after the Nile. It contains one-fifth of the world's fresh water.

The Amazon is not a place for paddling! Piranhas have razor-sharp teeth and a **shoal** of them can tear the flesh from an animal in minutes. Anaconda's are one of the largest types of snake in the world – they live in the river, hunting at night, attacking large creatures like goats that come to drink in the shallow water. Black caiman crocodiles can grow over five metres long.

an anaconda

Protecting the rainforest

Huge areas of the rainforest have been chopped down for wood, and to clear space to grow crops for food. This is called deforestation. Governments and other groups around the world are working very hard to slow this down.

There are many reasons why we need to protect the Amazon.

The rainforest makes a big difference to our weather. The warm air from the forest carries tiny droplets of water into the air. This creates rain, which helps to cool down the **global** temperature. Without the rainforest, there'd be less rain, and plants and crops wouldn't grow so well.

As the trees grow, they **absorb** a large amount of the world's carbon dioxide (CO_2). This is a gas which comes from burning coal, natural gas and oils. Whenever we drive a car, or go on an aeroplane, we add more carbon dioxide to the air.

Scientists know that the world has already warmed up because of all the carbon dioxide we're putting into the air. This is called global warming.

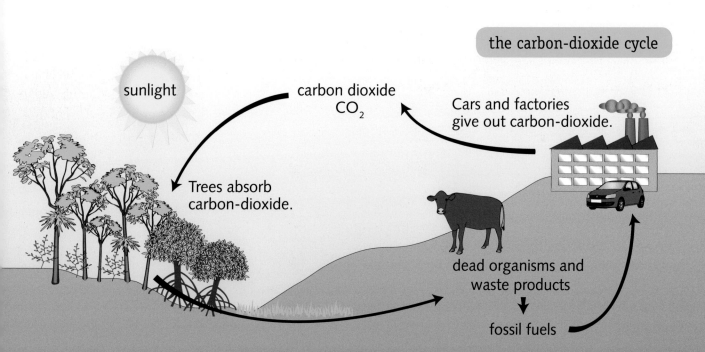

the carbon-dioxide cycle

sunlight

carbon dioxide
CO_2

Cars and factories
give out carbon-dioxide.

Trees absorb
carbon-dioxide.

dead organisms and
waste products

fossil fuels

If the Amazon rainforest gets smaller, it'll store less carbon dioxide. This could mean that the weather may get even warmer, causing problems for plants, animals and people.

The Amazon contains some of the world's most unusual wildlife. Many species are already **endangered**; many more are still undiscovered. Looking after the rainforest means saving the lives of all these **unique** living creatures and plants.

Some species of glass frogs are endangered.

Spotlight on Brazil!

As Brazil prepares for the Olympics, Rio and its beaches are being cleaned up. More money is being spent on making buses and trains run better. It's hoped that the Olympics will help improve some things for the people who live in Rio.

Many of the people who work in Brazil's offices and factories are young, energetic and excited about making it a better place to live for everyone.

The more changes made today, the brighter Brazil's future will be.

Glossary

abolished   stopped, brought to an end

absorb   soak up

climate   the usual weather in a place

endangered   at risk of dying out

equator   the imaginary circle around the Earth, halfway between the North and South Poles

eye-catching   very noticeable

fertile   good for growing plants and crops

flamboyant   showy and dramatic

foraging   searching for food

founded   set up or created

global   to do with the whole of the Earth

grieving   feeling very sad

humid   damp and steamy

illegally   against the law

independent   separate, able to support itself

metropolis   a large city

motto   a short saying

native   coming from a particular place

official   agreed and approved by the people in charge

republic   a place that is run by an elected government, not by a king or queen

settlers   people who arrive in a country from somewhere else and then stay

shoal   a large group (usually fish)

smuggled   taken in or out of a country, against the law

sociable   friendly, good with groups of people

sprawling   spread out in a disorganised way

unique   one of a kind

varied   different or changing

Index

Let's go to Brazil!

The Amazon rainforest – take a guided walk through the hot, steamy jungle.

Brasília – see the capital, and its incredible modern buildings

Try some typical food and sip an exotic fruit juice.

Cruise down the Amazon River but watch out for crocodiles!

Enjoy the white sandy beaches of Rio de Janiero

Visit a busy favela

Join in the samba as the dancers pass by.

Watch a football match at one of the World Cup stadiums

31

Ideas for reading

Written by Clare Dowdall, PhD
Lecturer and Primary Literacy Consultant

Reading objectives:

- read books that are structured in different ways
- ask questions to improve understanding
- identify how language, structure and presentation contribute to meaning
- retrieve and record information from non-fiction

Spoken language objectives/requirements:

- ask relevant questions to extend their understanding and knowledge

Curriculum links: Geography – locational knowledge; place knowledge; human and physical geography

Resources: Globe, atlas or ICT world map, whiteboards, ICT for research, art materials/ICT for making adverts

Build a context for reading

- Look at the front cover and read the blurb. Prepare children for reading by asking them to talk about one thing that they know about Brazil.
- Help children to locate Brazil and South America on a world map or globe. Discuss how it is different to the UK.
- Look at the contents page together. Ask children to explain how this information book is structured and which chapter headings interest them the most.

Understand and apply reading strategies

- Turn to pp2–3. Challenge children to play "Fact find". In pairs, how many facts can they find and list on a whiteboard, in two minutes. Discuss how we can find facts when we read. Share strategies for finding important facts, e.g. skimming and scanning, then close reading for understanding.
- Look closely at the illustrations and fact boxes on pp2–3. Check that children understand that these features add information and work with the text.